Working children

Brigid McConville

Macdonald

A MACDONALD BOOK

© Donna Bailey Ltd, 1988

First published in Great Britain in 1988 by
Macdonald & Co. (Publishers) Ltd
London and Sydney
A Pergamon Press plc company

ISBN 0 356 13739 2

Editor Donna Bailey
Production Controller Julia Mather
Picture Research Caroline Smith
Designed by Jim Weaver

Printed in Portugal by
Printer Portuguesa

Macdonald & Co. (Publishers) Ltd
Greater London House
Hampstead Road
London NW1 7QX

BRITISH LIBRARY
CATALOGUING IN PUBLICATION DATA
McConville, Brigid
    Working Children. – (Children in Conflict)
    1. Children – Employment
    I. Title   II. Series
    331.3'1   HD6231
    ISBN 0-356-13739-2

Credits

Aldus Archive: 7t, 15, 40.
Format: 36; Sue Darlow/Format: 17b, 20, 23; Jenny
    Matthews/Format: 17t, 22l; Maggie Murray/Format:
    22r; Brenda Prince/Format: 29t, 29br, 41.
Sally and Richard Greenhill: cover tr, 5t, 12, 13, 14l, 19,
    26r, 28-9b, 31b, 33b, 35, 38, 39b.
John and Penny Hubley: 30.
Mansell Collection: 6, 7b, 8, 9.
Archie Miles: 11t.
Simon Miles: cover bl, 37b.
Popperfoto: 5b, 10, 11b, 14r, 25, 26l, 31t, 37t.
Rex Features: 4, 16, 24, 27, 32, 34, 39t.
Frank Spooner Picture Agency: 18, 21, 33t.

Contents

Working all over the world

Children have always worked, and all over the world today they are still working.

Children do important work at home – cooking, collecting firewood, fetching water from wells and minding younger children. They do important work in gardens and fields – weeding, planting, sowing seeds and harvesting. They tend animals too, looking after sheep, goats, cows, pigs and chickens.

Many other children work in factories, sometimes on huge production lines, sometimes in small workshops making crafts. There are about 150 million children across the world who do some kind of work. The vast majority of them – 98 per cent – are in the developing world.

Much of the time, the fact that children are working means that they are being exploited. Adults are treating them unfairly. Sometimes employers are cruel and brutal to child workers, too. Some employers make children labour for long hours, without paying them properly or taking care of their needs. These adults put greed and their own personal profit before the lives of children.

Because they have to work, child labourers may never have the time for play or lessons which they need to develop their own selves. And some children have to work as soon as they can walk. Usually this kind of children's work is against the law. Yet it still goes on, both in the Third World and the rich West.

Some kinds of child labour are very shocking. Many children today live as slaves, forced into doing jobs that are dangerous and damaging. Sometimes they have no choice about doing terrible jobs: if they didn't work they would die of starvation, or their family would.

In some countries where poverty is widespread, children are sold by their parents to work for other people. These parents may not be able to feed their own children, and hope that their new 'boss' will give their child a better way of life. Tragically, greedy and unscrupulous adults often exploit these children. Some end up being abused sexually.

But work is not always bad for children. As long as adults don't misuse their power over children, the right kinds of work at the right age can be interesting, challenging and good fun. Children are people too, and most people love the independence and pleasure of a job well done – plus some cash into the bargain!

Left This fifteen-year-old girl is working in a Hong Kong 'sweat-shop' – a factory which pays her very little money for a lot of hard work. On her circular machine she makes the neck portions for knitwear. But it's hot and stuffy in the sweat-shop, and because she works such long hours, she doesn't get any fresh air, daylight or exercise. Doing the same repetitive job all day long under the strip lighting is not only boring – it's bad for her eyesight and her health. And because she's working at such a young age, her chances of getting a good education are over.

Left His back may be sore at the end of the day, but this Scottish school boy looks like he's enjoying the potato harvest. He's working with his friends in the fresh air, and although he wouldn't want to do this all year round, he knows it's only temporary and that soon he'll be back in the classroom. 'Picking tatties' will also bring him some money of his own. And of course its a nice change to be allowed a bit of time off school!

Right She's at the age to play with dolls. But instead, this little Indian girl from Peru has got a real live baby to feed, carry, dress and change. She won't get paid for minding her little brother, but by looking after him, she gives her mother freedom to go out and earn money for the family. It also means this girl has got a grown-up woman's responsibilities when she's still only small herself. In some ways her childhood is already over.

Our past – the Third World's present?

Ragged children mining coal in darkness and danger? Children sweating in the fields and factories instead of going to school? 'It would never happen in America or Britain,' you might think. But it did happen, and not so long ago. In some cases, it still does.

Life for children was very different before the Industrial Revolution which completely changed the modern world. In those days, many children started work just as soon as they were able to. Even at three and four years old, the youngest members of the family had responsibilities.

In the Middle Ages, the idea of childhood as we think of it didn't exist. Children were simply seen as small adults, and they were expected to do a share of the work just like anyone else. Children and adults mixed

Above In past centuries, European children often worked just as any other adult. In these pictures of the hay harvest, men and women, girls and boys are sharing in all the jobs. The young girl rakes and stacks the hay just like her mother and the other adults. It is a boy's job to hold and ride the farm horse, just as much as an older man's. The boy could be the son of the family, or he could be an apprentice sent to live with and work for this family.

together at all times – working together and playing together.

Most children were kept at home until about the age of eight. Then they went to live with another family as an apprentice – a kind of junior worker or servant. This seems harsh to us today. But in the past, children were not seen as belonging to just one small family. They belonged to the whole community.

The apprentice system was also the best way for children to learn a skill, a trade or a craft. Education was not something you got in school. Instead, children learned by working with older people, who would pass on their knowledge to the young generation. Of course, some children had happier lives in their master's house than others did, depending on how kind he was. Discipline was strict, and apprentices were often whipped.

The whole family group plus apprentices or servants lived and worked together at home. Many families farmed a small-holding and kept a few animals which the children would help to care for, such as pigs, chickens, or perhaps a cow.

Children were also expected to share the work of the small industries which in those days were run from home, such as lace-making, stocking-knitting and chain-making.

Right It is nothing new for children to work in factories – as this picture of a sixteenth-century armour workshop shows. One boy carries a heavy load, another files down a metal breast-plate while another inspects a piece of armour. The artist's drawing shows the belief of the time that children were just like adults, only smaller. Here, the children work like adults, look like mini-adults and even dress in clothes no different from those of the adults.

Left In Britain's mines children once hauled coal tubs and worked as 'trappers', opening the doors for the tubs to pass through. Yet the hardship and poverty suffered by the millions of child labourers in Britain's past was in contrast to the wealth and luxury of the ruling classes. Reformers began objecting to a system which made children from four years of age spend over fourteen hours a day down a mineshaft. This cartoon is from the magazine *Punch* in 1843.

Victorian values

As the eighteenth-century came to a close, the old ways of working within family and community groups were swept away by great changes in society.

In the countryside, the common land which every labourer had once been allowed to use, was taken over by the wealthy owners of huge country estates. It was shut off from ordinary people, who then had nowhere to graze a cow or some sheep.

Meanwhile the Industrial Revolution with its new machinery began the modern factory system. This put an end to the tradition of people working at home in cottage industries. Instead, adults and children alike were forced to work in the factories and mines, in dangerous and degrading jobs. Because adults weren't paid enough to feed their children, the children had to work too – for even less money.

The Victorian businessmen wanted child workers because they were so cheap and so plentiful. Yet children were treated like slaves. They worked such long hours that bosses would whip them in order to keep them awake at their jobs.

Below Whole families worked in the big new factories of the Industrial Revolution. Yet, like these sad brothers saying goodbye, they were divided from each other at work. Strict overseers often beat the children to keep them hard at work. Ragged, starving and exhausted children had to keep up with their jobs simply to survive. Here, one boy's job is to crawl and sweep underneath the whirring factory machines.

Above It was a terrible life for the thousands of boys who were made to climb and clean chimneys during the nineteenth-century. In those days, every home had a fireplace and a chimney to clean. But 'sweeps' sometimes suffocated to death in the narrow, soot-filled chimneys. If they refused to keep climbing up such a chimney, cruel bosses would light fires beneath them. Only in 1873 did the British statesman Lord Shaftesbury convince Parliament that using children to sweep the chimneys should be stopped.

Left These two girls are sifting brick dust through sieves. The scene is taken from an English brickyard in 1871. It is backbreaking and dirty work, during which they can't help breathing in the clouds of dust. Yet it doesn't earn them enough money to buy shoes, or to replace their rags with decent clothes.

Most factory owners employed children, usually from the age of eight. However, some children went to work when they were only five years old.

In the mid nineteenth-century, half of all textile factory workers were under eighteen. These children worked for about fourteen to sixteen hours a day (not counting mealtimes) under the strict rule of their bosses.

Some orphans and the children of widows were sent to mill-owners in the north of England during the 1820s. The children were paid about two shillings (ten new pence) for over 72 hours work.

In the rural areas too, child workers were exploited in small industries, like lace-making, straw-plaiting and glue-making.

Here they worked at even younger ages than in the factories, and for even lower wages. Many other children lived as outcasts on the streets of London and other cities. They survived by running errands, polishing shoes, sweeping streets, guarding horses, and through prostitution.

Only slowly did people begin to see this exploitation of children as immoral, and during the nineteenth-century various laws banned the worst cruelties. In 1802, it became illegal in Britain to make children work more than twelve hours a day, and in 1833 the Factory Act stopped the employment of children under nine years old. Yet there was still a long, long way to go ...

Changing childhood

In the nineteenth-century, social reformers like Lord Shaftesbury campaigned to improve the appalling lives of many working children. But progress was slow. Many people were so used to seeing children suffering hardship that they accepted it as part of life.

There was also a common view in Victorian times that everyone had their place. People who saw the system as unjust and who tried to change things, faced severe punishments. And so for a long time, privileged children continued to enjoy leisure and education, while poor children were condemned to a life of menial work.

There was also strong resistance to change from the factory owners. They were quite happy to be making a fat profit out of children. Parents too were reluctant to see their children taken out of the work force. Often their own wages were so low that they needed their children to earn money.

Yet concern about cruelty to child workers was growing. In the 1860s Charles Kingsley wrote *The Waterbabies*, a book which told about the tragic lives of the child chimney sweeps. Soon after, the law was changed to ban the use of children for sweeping chimneys.

However, child labour didn't come to an end just because people became more sympathetic and decided it was wrong. Progress in technology had allowed manufacturers to improve their machines. This meant they could use more machines instead of cheap child labour.

Below This twelve-year-old boy is a 'half-timer'. He works on this machine at the mill for half of the day, and spends the other half in the factory school. The photograph was taken in 1920. Fifty years earlier and he would have got no schooling; fifty years later he would not be allowed to do this work because of changes in the law about child labour. Gradually, education was becoming more important than work in children's lives.

But it was in the 1870s that the most important change occurred in Britain. A new law said that all children under the age of ten had to go to school as full-time pupils. It was this which finally put an end to the widespread use of child labour in Britain. Education became the ladder on which children could escape from a life of hardship and drudgery.

And as the standard of living generally improved into the twentieth-century, people were able to show more care and concern for the health and welfare of their children.

Right Attitudes to childhood have changed with the times. By the Victorian era, a long period of education was thought to be a good thing – for the children of families who could afford it. This was partly because the modern business world was becoming more complex. Middle and upper-class children had a lot of things to learn if they wanted to be successful bosses. But it took many more years before a decent education was seen as a good thing for poor children too.

Right A hundred years ago, most middle-class households employed a team of servants to do the messy, time-consuming jobs of cleaning and cooking. These girls had a life of stern, obedient hard work. They could never earn enough to escape from the life of a servant. Unless they married, they might live and die working in the same household. Servant girls were only allowed home once a year on Mothering Sunday. That's the origin of the modern Mothers' Day.

Britain today – still labouring on

Above All over the world children work in agriculture, and this is seen as a normal part of country life. These British children picking peas are no exception. Children in Britain can legally work on farms from the age of 13 for 86 pence an hour. But many younger children work in agriculture too, either under their parents' supervision or under 'gangmasters'. They often get paid less than the legal minimum wage.

The number of child workers in Britain is much higher than most people think. It is about two and a half million – and going up.

Almost half of all teenagers below school-leaving age have some kind of paid job. Newspaper rounds and milk delivery are the most typical jobs for children, followed by work in shops. Then comes farming, and work in stables, kennels and jobs with various other animals.

Although the cruelty and exploitation of child work in Victorian times has mostly gone, there are still reasons to be concerned about child workers in Britain. Children as young as eleven are working up to seven hours a day in factories. They make shoes and leather goods. Others are working on building sites, in factories, in garages and abattoirs. Many children in tourist towns are working in hotels and pubs.

British children today work cleaning hospitals, processing vegetables and making furniture. It is often illegal for them to be employed in these jobs. Some children still work in conditions of slave labour in the 'rag trade' – making clothing in 'sweat-shops'.

Like the sweeps of past centuries, children have been employed to crawl through narrow ducts in a factory. This was only found out when one boy fell and was injured. The factory was prosecuted and fined.

One schoolboy was working six days a week in a shirt factory until he was totally exhausted. 'My dad's out of work' he said, 'and I don't get much pocket-money, so I just had to get back to work.' Another boy described the same factory as 'cramped and filthy, and adults are always yelling at you.'

The regulations protecting children from harm, exploitation and injury are often not enforced. A third of child workers have accidents in their jobs. A third also suffer from being very tired. Yet their pay is often less than £1.00 an hour. Sometimes it's as little as 17p an hour.

Above This babysitter has got her two young charges well under control. But minding children can be very hard work. Yet it's not well paid, and it doesn't get recorded as an official 'job'. Millions of children in Britain do jobs that aren't seen as real employment. A half million women are homeworkers, doing piece-rate jobs at home, but no one knows how many children 'help' their mothers with such work.

Most children work for fewer than ten hours a week. But some do full time jobs as well as going to school. The more paid work children do, the less time they have to study, and the more their schoolwork suffers.

However, when children's work is kept within sensible and legal limits it can benefit youngsters. It gives them work experience and responsibility, which helps develop their personalities and self-worth. The extra money is worth having too!

Right Work in shops is common amongst British teenagers. This boy's job is to stack shelves in the supermarket. Children under fifteen aren't supposed to be employed in this kind of work. There are also restrictions on the hours that children can work in shops. But many do work in family-run businesses, even when it is against the law. Sometimes this is because parents simply don't realize that they are operating against the rules.

The rest of the West

Child labour is not just a problem in Britain but in other developed countries of Europe and in the United States of America as well. Just as in Britain, unscrupulous employers in the western world take advantage of the fact that children are cheaper and easier to exploit than adults.

In many cities in Europe children work in small industries, in shops and 'helping' their mothers at home with piece-work. In the Italian city of Naples, for instance, some children are apprentices from the age of ten in the shoe-making industry.

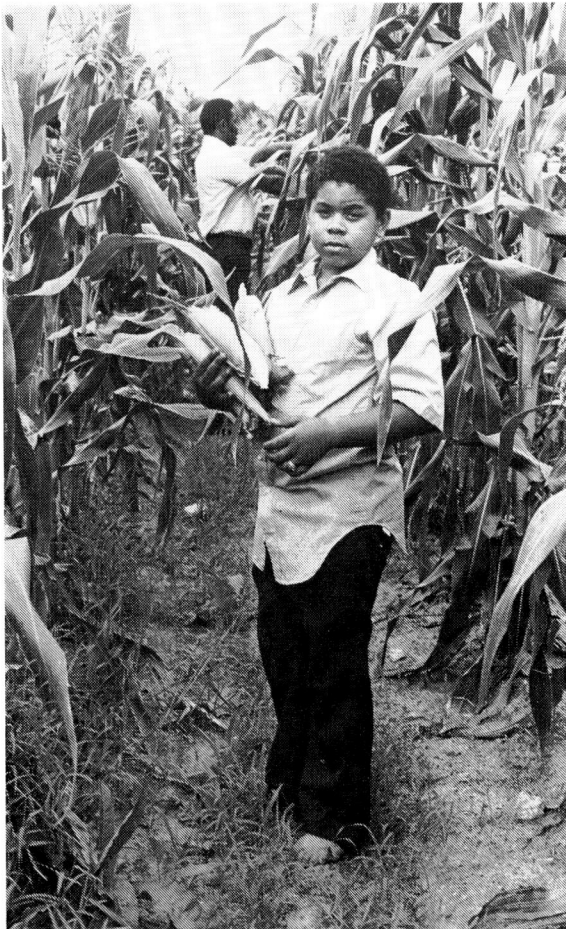

Above It's hard work for this Sicilian boy driving a mule and cart. Yet he is making an important contribution to the livelihood of his whole family. In Sicily, nearly half of all fourteen-year-olds are truant from school because they are needed to work on family farms or to earn some cash. Almost a quarter of a million children in Sicily have jobs.

In Lisbon, Portugal, children aged nine to fourteen work up to fifteen hours a day for as little as £27 a month. They spend the day in basements and garages, stitching shoes or sewing clothes. They are served soup on the job so that they won't stop work for a lunch break.

In Spain, children in tourist resorts are often seen stacking the shelves of small family stores with tins and groceries. In Ireland too, some children work late hours 'helping' their parents who run shops, pubs or hotels.

In Italy, a country which has perhaps the highest number of working children in Europe, small children may work all day tending flocks of animals in the fields. Children in poor parts of Yugoslavia are being sold by their parents to other adults. Then they are taken to camps near Rome where they are trained to work as thieves and beggars. The adults take the money they get.

But it's not just the poor parts of the West who use working children. In rich, industrial West Germany, some 20,000 children are working in industry. America, the most

Above Picking corn in North Carolina USA is hot work for this American boy. His family probably needs the extra cash he is earning. Meanwhile he is missing out on the education which could help him to get a better job in the future. But it's right now that the family is short of money. Perhaps by the end of the season they will be able to buy him some new shoes.

Above No, it's not Victorian England – this girl is working in a cotton mill in the Southern States of the USA. The year is 1900. America inherited England's tradition of child labour with all its worst abuses. Until this century, children worked in terrible conditions in coal mines and textile factories. And as in Britain today, millions of children still work, legally and illegally.

powerful country in the world, still has millions of child labourers. They work mostly in agriculture, where they make up a quarter of the paid work force. This is despite the fact that fifty years ago a law was passed to ban children under sixteen from working.

As in other countries, it tends to be the families of the poorest people in America whose children are exploited as cheap labour. Millions of children in migrant families – often Mexicans – work in the fields with their parents. Although they work in the open air, the work is hard, the hours are long and the pay is low. As a result, these fields of migrant workers with their children are often called 'Blue-sky Sweat-shops'.

South of the Equator

For most children in the world, work is not a matter of adding to their pocket-money – it's a matter of life and death. Their families are so poor that even the smallest child must contribute, sometimes as soon as they can walk.

Almost all of the world's labouring children live in the developing world, and most of them work in agriculture. Many are never paid in money for what they do. Their work is to help with growing food on the family small-holding, or looking after the animals which are a source of food.

Other children in the developing world work for wages, doing a wide variety of jobs. Children in the Third World – especially girls – also do a lot of domestic work at home. This doesn't earn cash, but it does give parents the opportunity to do other kinds of work. It is mostly girls who do these 'invisible', unpaid jobs of cooking, cleaning and minding their younger brothers and sisters.

Many other children in the developing world are slaves, sold by their parents after crop failures. In Thailand, trainloads of children arrive in the city of Bangkok to be sold for less than £100 each. The money is supposed to be the child's wages for a year, but at the end of the year, parents don't get their children back again.

The Third World is also plagued by a system called debt bondage. This isn't much different from slavery. Many children have to work without wages to pay off the debts of their parents, or even their grandparents. Often the adults have been trapped into those debts by agreeing to pay back loans at an impossible rate of interest.

Then there is the whole range of jobs done by children all over the developing world which are never officially counted as employment. These include anything from running errands and guarding parked cars, to stealing, prostitution and picking through rubbish. The world's most destitute children do anything they can to survive.

In many ways, the plight of child labourers in the developing world today is like that of

Above Picking through the rubbish at the town dump isn't work which gets paid – it's work just to survive. At this scene in Brazil, boys are working together with men and women to collect tin cans out of the rubbish. These are gathered into the basket, and later beaten flat to be made into other metal objects – like water cans. The 'new' cans are then sold for cash.

Left It's a heavy load to carry and a long way up the hill for this little girl. She is working in the Nicaraguan coffee harvest carrying sacks of coffee beans – just like the adults coming up behind her. The crop she's lifting fetches high prices in the markets of the western world. Yet although she's doing a grown-up job which earns her employer a lot of money, she's only getting a child's pay.

children in the West 150 years ago. The richer nations have 'exported' many of the problems. There may not be so many child labourers in the West today, but we still buy and sell and profit from the products made by children overseas who are forced to work because of poverty.

Above These are the children of migrant workers in India. Their job is to prepare the pile of cotton flowers for cross-pollination. They work sitting on the ground in the open air, with nothing to shade them from the sun. It's unskilled, repetitive work. No tools or equipment are needed. The work done by their sons' fingers adds to the earnings of their parents, who are busy doing other jobs in the cotton fields.

Where East meets West

Millions of children in the developing world make products which people of the rich West buy. While this system often makes big profits for the people who employ these child workers, it brings few profits to the children themselves.

Take Lakshmi, a twelve-year-old girl who lives and works on a tea plantation in India. Her working day starts at 4.00 am when she helps her mother to get breakfast for the family. Lakshmi starts picking tea at 6.00 a.m. and works for ten hours. When she gets home she collects water from the communal tap, and after the evening meal of rice and lentils, she does the washing up. Then she washes the family's clothes.

India has 44 million child workers, the biggest number in the world. Thousands of them work on tea plantations. Half of the children get drunk on the local rice alcohol, a sign of how unhappy their lives are. Because the plantations are so isolated, workers cannot escape, and even have to buy their food from the plantation owners.

Below These Chinese children are gathering the resin from the heads of poppy flowers. The resin forms the raw material of drugs like opium and heroin. Drug users in the western world will pay huge sums of money for these. But it is the drug dealers who make the fortunes. These children won't make their fortunes from the drug trade. They are just the innocent first link in a long chain of exploitation which stretches from East to West.

Above What could be more cosy than a nice pot of tea? But as we pour ourselves another cup, few of us think where the tea leaves have come from. It's disturbing to know that they often come from the hands of overworked, badly treated children who are paid just enough to keep them alive. This little Indian girl works all day long for just a few pence.

Below Hunched over their sewing machines in cramped conditions, these two girls in a Hong Kong sweat-shop don't even have the comfort of being able to face each other as they work. The pile of jeans they have been stitching may be sold in shops in the West. But these girls won't reap any of the profits – just a very low wage for some very long hours of work. The less they get paid, the more their employers can make out of them.

The children are especially in demand at tea-harvest time, because their soft, nimble fingers are best for picking the leaves without damaging them. This ensures that India's biggest customers for tea – Britain and the USSR – can have the best quality product.

Millions of other children all over the developing world also produce food for us in the West, as well as carpets for our floors, clothes, toys and a range of other goods.

In Pakistan and India, children are so much in demand to work as carpet weavers that they are sometimes kidnapped. The good eyesight and small fingers of children mean they are quick at tying the hundreds of tiny knots per square inch which makes a

good carpet. To a greedy employer, child labour is a godsend.

In Thailand, children work in slave conditions making clothes. In one 'rag-trade sweat-shop' in Bangkok, 250 girls work from 8.00 a.m. to 11 p.m., seven days a week. They sleep feet to feet on the rough floor of a dormitory, where there are no fans and where the open toilets are often blocked. The jeans you bought in your high street shop may have come from there.

Britain and America have laws which ban this kind of exploitation of children (although it still goes on illegally in some cases). But some employers simply get around the law by using child labour in other, poorer countries.

Children of the street

Regianni is sixteen years old. She has been working and living on the streets of Sao Paulo, the capital of Brazil, since she left home at the age of eight. She ran away because of family quarrels and problems.

Regianni started committing petty crimes with other children when she was only about six. By the age of eight she was living permanently on the streets, where adults used her to carry out crimes for them. She went from picking pockets, to robbing houses and selling drugs – and ended up committing six murders.

Regianni was born in one of Sao Paulo's terrible slums where half of the city's population now lives. More than half a million children there fend for themselves on the streets – begging, stealing, cleaning cars, polishing shoes, selling goods on the streets. Others turn to prostitution, robbery and more serious crimes, doing whatever jobs they can to survive.

Above At five years old, this Indian girl's job is to beg for money. She sits holding her baby sister – perhaps to get sympathy, perhaps because there is no one else to care for the child. The place this young beggar has chosen is a picturesque old mosque in Delhi. She hopes she will be seen by tourists with some spare cash in their pockets who will give her some money.

When the street children are caught, they are punished by being locked in grim institutions. Here they may be subject to abuse and cruelty. The religious organizations and charities who try to defend them say that there is little sympathy or help for their situation. Local people fear and despise the street children, in case they are robbed themselves.

Some of these street children still have links with their homes and give the money they earn to help support their families. But other street children have run away from families where they faced poverty, abuse and neglect.

It's a massive, international problem. Some forty million children around the world work – and live – on the streets. Mostly they are victims of a quickly-changing world, in which people looking for work are moving from country communities to huge cities. Poverty, and the harshness of life in the slums, puts so much strain on these people that family life often breaks down.

The problem is most obvious in South America, where rapid industrialization has put an end to traditional ways of working. In addition, repressive military rulers have ignored the plight of the poor. But many countries have their own street children – including those in the rich West. These days it's not unusual to see children begging and stealing in the capital cities of Europe.

Right The driver of this shiny car in the streets of Peru doesn't even get out of his seat. He just has to stick his leg out of the car door to get his shoes polished up. He knows he will only have to pay a bit of loose change for the service, so it's no big deal to him. But for the boy who kneels on the grass verge by his feet, this job is his bread and butter.

Below It's not just the poor countries of the world which have children making a living on the streets. These gypsy children in Paris work in a group: some of them distract and harass a tourist, while the others pick her pockets. Of course it is against the law, but as children, they can't be punished as severely as adults for their crime. Sometimes child thieves are organized and controlled by adult criminals who take the profits for themselves.

Cinderellas in the home

Murielle is a young French girl who came to Britain as an au pair, expecting to do a little housekeeping and babysitting in exchange for room and board, and a chance to learn English.

Instead she found herself slaving for an upper-class family, who made her cook, clean, iron, serve them food and mind their baby. She was only allowed one hour a week to learn English. Eventually, after losing over six kilos in weight, she walked out.

Murielle is a modern example of how many girls are still exploited in the privacy of the home. For it is girls who – the world over – are still expected to do the lowly, boring and unpaid jobs of housework.

Very little is known about this kind of child labour, because it doesn't directly produce any goods or make any money. Yet millions of girl workers live like slaves as domestic servants in homes all over the world. It is a powerless and much exploited existence for many isolated children. These girls are virtual prisoners in the homes where they work, with no money or friends to help if they want to escape.

Above She has taken the job of 'au pair' in an English home, hoping to improve her English and to see something of life in a foreign country. But all she can see at the moment is another pile of washing up. Meanwhile, the child she is supposed to be a companion to sits watching television with his mother in the background. She feels like a real Cinderella!

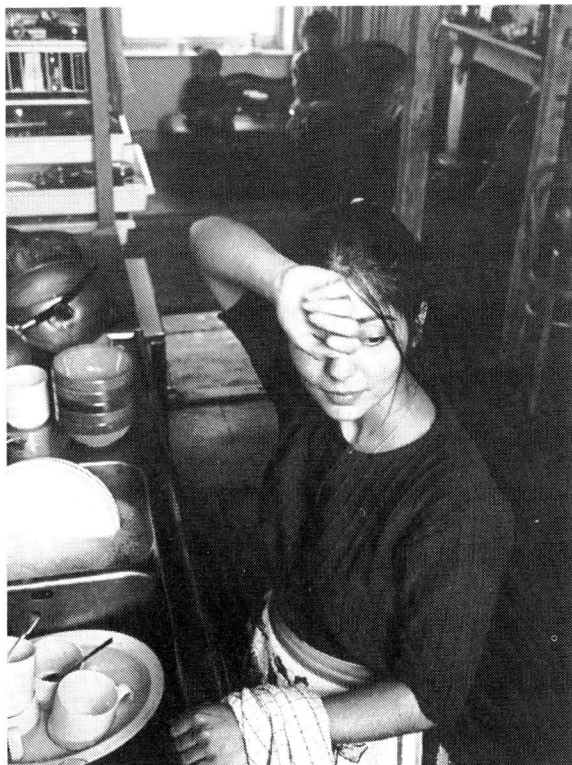

Left A big sister carries a bundle of washing on her head down the unpaved road. Her little sister, carrying the plastic bucket, has come to help her do the laundry. This is Nicaragua, where few people can afford labour-saving inventions like washing machines. As a result, domestic work can take up many more hours than in the West. And in many countries of the world, girls are needed to help with the day to day tasks of running the home from an early age.

Left Plenty of pots and pans for this Indian girl to wash up. At the age of fourteen she is employed as a domestic servant by a New Delhi family. The lady of the house is keeping an eye on her work as she rinses the utensils under the tap. It's much the same kind of job that many English servant girls did in the 'old days'.

Take Peru, where many children of Indians from the mountain areas are sent to the city of Lima. Here they are taken into domestic service from the age of seven upwards. Their parents allow them to be 'adopted' by wealthy families, in the hope that they will be educated and given decent work. Yet these girls are paid very low wages – about a third of the pay of an unskilled labourer in Peru. They have few rights, and may have to work for 16 hours a day. The men of the families may make sexual advances to them, but if they become pregnant, the girls are thrown out onto the streets.

Domestic servants often eat different food at different times from the families they work for. These girls may have nowhere to sleep except for the kitchen.

In South Africa, black girls from the age of eleven often work as servants or 'nannies' for white families. However, there are no laws to protect these children, who can be called upon to work at any time of day or night.

Selling children's bodies

Above These young prostitutes in the Philippines are smiling and posing for the camera. They spend a lot of time in night-clubs and bars trying to attract business from tourists, hence the make-up and the clothes. But the job of making your body available to whoever can pay for it is not a glamorous one. These children suffer damage to their health, self-esteem and emotions. They risk pregnancy and serious diseases. And because prostitution is looked down on, they are never really accepted in the rest of society.

All over the world, children sell their labour – either for pocket-money or for sheer survival. But sometimes it is not children's labour as we normally think of it that adults want to buy. Instead they want the use of children's bodies.

Paying a child money for the use of her pretty face in an advertisement or a play can be relatively harmless – provided she is well cared for and her education is not neglected.

However, many children are used as models or actresses in pornography. This trade in magazines and pictures about sex is often violent and degrading. Yet it is an international industry that is worth millions of pounds and which is linked to the Mafia and the drug smuggling trade.

Other children are forced into selling their bodies for sex as prostitutes. Some are sold or kidnapped by adults to be used in the vice industry. Of all the forms of child labour which exploit young girls and boys, these are perhaps the most distressing and damaging.

Not much is known about child prostitution, but it seems to be a problem in the rich West as much as it is in the developing world. Some 10,000 children are prostitutes in Paris, while a million children live this way in the USA. Children usually turn to prostitution because of poverty, or because they are addicted to drugs and need money.

Many children end up working as prostitutes after running away from unhappiness at home, and then finding that they have no other way to survive. Many children have suffered sexual abuse in their own homes. Because they have been deeply hurt by this experience, they more easily become victims to even more exploitation by other adults.

In poor countries like Thailand, the Philippines, Latin and South America, children are sometimes sold or stolen for sex. Unscrupulous people known as child traders appear in poor countries where there have been recent disasters like crop failures or earthquakes. They pretend to be relief workers or adoption agents who want to help children. Instead, they put them into a life of prostitution or pornography.

Apart from the risks of violence and disease, to be used by strangers for sex without love or consideration causes terrible emotional pain. Young prostitutes may never be able to find happiness in loving, caring relationships of their own. They may never be able to trust or care for someone because of the damage done to them as children.

And now child prostitutes everywhere are falling victim to the killer illness AIDS. The use of prostitutes in developing countries by visiting Western businessmen is one of the reasons for the rapid spread of AIDS around the world.

Above By the age of eight, the little American girl in the middle of the picture is an experienced star. She now works regularly as a professional entertainer and model. Her career began when she was only three. As a tiny tot she modelled clothes for catalogues. At the age of four she was making television advertisements. At five she was singing in a night-club, and now she sings in the Broadway musical hit *Annie*. Her pretty face and singing talent have been used to make a lot of money. But was it really with her best interests at heart – and was she old enough to choose this career for herself when she was only three years old?

A matter of definition

It's not always easy to draw the line between 'work' and other kinds of activity – like 'helping' or 'playing'.

For example, Susan's mother is making a pair of curtains. She cuts out the material while Susan tacks and pins the pieces of cloth. Most people would say that the mother was working but that Susan was 'helping'. Most of us would think it was a good thing for a girl to help her mother with a job like this.

But what if Susan was making curtains in a Hong Kong factory for wages, instead of in her home without pay? We would think of her as 'working' – and we would probably think this was a bad thing.

Our ideas about the meaning of work have been strongly affected by history. Before the Industrial Revolution, there wasn't such a big gap between home and work. But these days 'going to work' means going to the office or the factory – or anywhere except home.

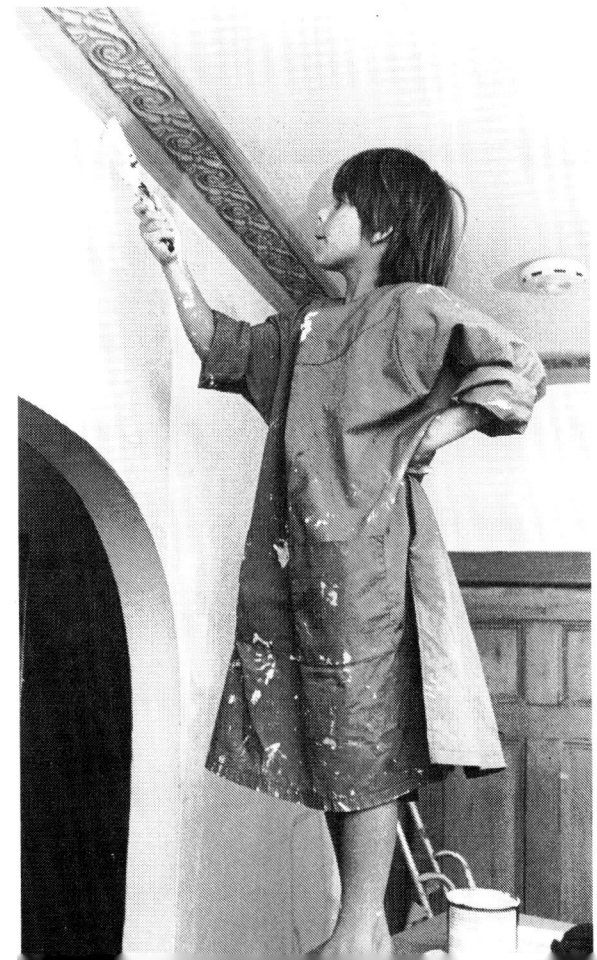

Above Soft, sweet and cuddly, this little black lamb would be a dream pet for many a western girl or boy. But this boy in Kashmir is doing more than hugging his pet lamb: he is doing his job as a shepherd. For him, caring for an animal is not just a fun part of childhood. It's not something he will be expected to grow out of as he gets older. Instead, learning to look after and to understand animals is a big part of his education for the work of adult life. He won't have any examination results or other qualifications on paper, but he will be trained and experienced in minding sheep before he is much older.

Right Painting and decorating takes a lot of concentration from this young girl. A foot wrong and she could have quite a serious fall, or knock a can of paint all over the floor. Which is why, if she were ten years older, she could be paid well to do this job professionally in someone else's home. But in western countries, children of her age are thought of as too young to take full responsibility for work like this. Still, she is allowed to 'help' at home with the decorating – work she may want to do in her own house one day.

In the West, we tend to think of children as dependent and in need of protection – which is why we don't expect them to take on the adult burden of 'work'. To us, it seems almost as odd for children to work as it does for adults *not* to work.

Most children in Europe go to school for at least ten years without doing any 'work' – as we think of it. Suddenly, as soon as they leave school or college, they go into a totally different world of jobs for which they have no experience at all.

Contrast other countries and cultures where this divide between home and work has not happened. Our past is in many ways like the Third World's present. Most children of the developing world 'work' in agriculture, often with their family's crops or animals. They may be at home and 'at work' at the same time.

But where there is not such a strict division between adult and child, work and 'helping', growing up into the world of work is much more gradual. Unlike a western child, an African child doesn't have a pet gerbil to play with, because a gerbil has nothing to contribute to his home. Instead, he has a hen which lays eggs. He sells the eggs to buy more hens – and so he learns about adult life and work at an early age.

Right Is it work? Or is it play? The Dad in the picture is certainly working – but he's working in his own garden, without pay and because he wants to. His little boy is helping to do the same job. But because the child is small and is using a toy wheelbarrow, we call what he is doing 'play'. Yet it's also true in a way that the Dad is 'playing' at gardening and playing with his child. The child is also learning to 'work'. The names we give to activities like this tells a great deal about our attitudes to children and work.

The rights and wrongs of children's work

Is it damaging for children to work? When that work means that children are exploited, the answer is definitely yes. Most kinds of child work damages children by stunting their development, health and education. Some kinds of child work reduce children to slaves: they are the property of another person and have to work with no rights or rewards of their own.

But there are times when children can benefit from work. Children can learn from work, make some money, have some freedom – and have fun too. Work can bring responsibility and experience, which helps children to mature and develop.

In many ways, children in the West are now in the position that women have been in for centuries past. Women were seen as the property of men, and because they were thought of as weak, they must be protected and kept at home. Yet this was often just an excuse to keep women slaving away in the home for long hours without pay or status.

These days children are still seen by many as the property of their parents. We like to think of 'the family' as a sacred thing – in which parents would never take advantage of their children. Because of this ideal, we refuse to believe that parents can exploit their own children. But some parents do make their children work extremely hard in the home. For instance, a child can make beds at home unpaid. But the same child is not allowed to make beds in a hotel, and get paid for it.

The attitude in many developing countries seems more honest. There, many children have to work. For too many of them, that work is hard and damaging to the child. But for the lucky ones, work brings a certain amount of independence – and cash. Money is power, and when children have their own money, they have a say in their own lives. That seems like a revolutionary idea in the West. Here we tend to think that parents should have all the money and control in the family.

And because we see 'real' work as something that makes money, we tend to forget that work has other good things to offer: like friendship with workmates; like a sense of satisfaction in a job well done; like experience and contact with other people.

Children can learn and enjoy from all these aspects of work. As children who do voluntary work find out, work can be worth doing for its own sake.

Right He washes his parents' car every weekend and gets a bit added on to his pocket money. But is it right that he should get paid for doing this job? After all, his sister has been doing the washing up while he's been cleaning the car – but she doesn't get paid for her chores. Our ideas about work are closely linked with money. If you don't get paid, it's not seen as real work. But then a lot of traditional 'women's' work – and girl's work – is housework. That never gets paid – so its not seen as 'real' work. And because its not seen as 'real' work, it doesn't get paid.

Left These two cheerful girls are selling vegetables at the roadside in Manila in the Philippines. No doubt they are proud of their produce, which looks fresh and carefully laid out. Their work looks fun too – out in the open air, talking to people, providing food for the family table. Each girl is her own boss, with no one to order her about or shout at her. The girls like feeling grown-up and being trusted with a proper job. Then there's the nice bit of money to take home at the end of the day. But what about their future: perhaps they would be better off in school?

Below There's nothing like a good cup of tea! In this picture it's provided by a London schoolgirl working at her local drop-in centre for members of the public. This is voluntary work, with no wages at the end of the day. Yet money isn't everything, and this girl enjoys being helpful and friendly. It makes her feel good about herself to know she is useful and needed. She enjoys the chat with the older people too. And for the women having their tea, her work provides pleasure, refreshment and a sense of community. Is there anything wrong with that?

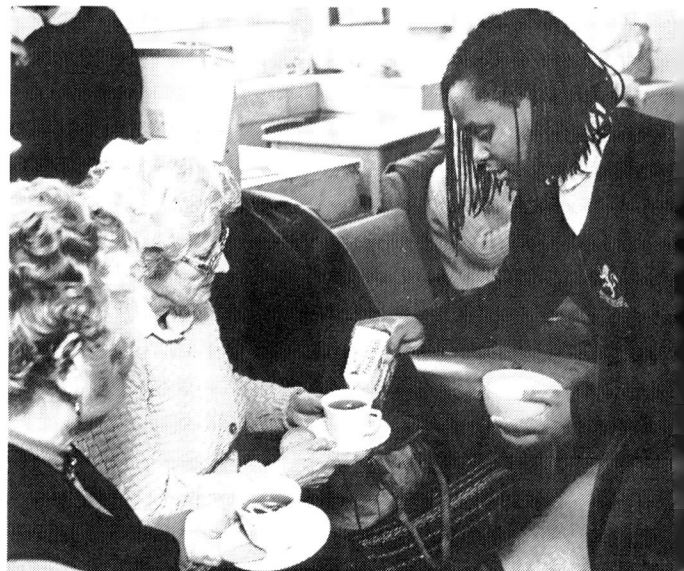

Why employers want children

Puttan is a seven-year-old Indian boy. He works for fifteen hours a day, every day of the week, weaving carpets in a remote village. He gets paid 25p a week. When he is finished his work, he is given rice and curry and left to sleep on a dirt floor.

It takes him a month to make a carpet, working with three other boys. They get paid a total of £4. The carpet is then sent to London, where it is sold in a top department store for thousands of pounds.

Thousands of boys like Puttan have been taken by force from their home villages. Many work without pay, and are starved and beaten to make them afraid to escape. If they try to run away they are whipped.

Right These Indian boys are weaving carpets. It's a job which children are good at because their small fingers are nimble enough to quickly tie thousands of tiny knots. The more the knots, the more valuable the carpets, which will be sold for huge sums of money in the West. But the children who make them will never see the profits. Some child weavers are kidnapped and then kept as 'bonded labour' or slaves. They are treated brutally and beaten if they try to run away.

The children are wanted by the carpet 'loom masters' because of their skill at tying tiny carpet knots, and because they can be kept and controlled more easily than adults. Their bosses are also keen to have these children because they can get away with paying them a pittance – or nothing at all.

In recent years, hundreds of children have been rescued by anti-slavery groups from this life of cruel exploitation in the carpet trade.

Employers in the West can't get away with exploiting children in their own countries on such a big scale because of the laws against it. But when they do employ child workers, it is often for the same reasons.

Children are cheaper to employ than adults. They are also more easily pushed around because they are physically smaller than adults, and less experienced in fighting for themselves. Children can be sacked easily, and taken on when needed. They are also in demand because employers can escape their obligations – like insurance.

Children don't usually organize themselves into trade unions to protect their rights. As a result, employers know that children won't cause them problems by going on strike, or demanding better work conditions. They are less likely to make a fuss over health and safety protection – which is all a saving for an unscrupulous boss.

It follows that in times of economic recession and unemployment, some employers find that children can make them easier profits than adults. And when parents are facing the desperation of unemployment and poverty, they are more likely to let their children go out to work.

Right This boy is just the kind of worker the farmer wants for the length of the turnip harvest. He's strong enough to carry the net full of vegetables, but needs no special skills. Unlike an adult, he can be paid a low wage, cash into his hand – without the farmer having to pay out national insurance contributions. And at the end of the harvest he can be laid off. No need for his boss to worry about work contracts or other legal obligations.

Above A thousand people in this crowd in Detroit, USA, are desperate for a job. But there are only a hundred vacancies, so the official on the platform tosses the application forms into the crowd for the lucky ones to catch. The company is filling the jobs of a hundred workers on strike – a tactic which completely ignores the demands of the workers and which many people believe is wrong and unjust. Yet jobs are now so hard to get that the company can get away with it. In this situation, when adults can't get work, children often have to work to bring some cash into their homes.

Health and safety at risk

Ten children in Britain were killed doing farm work in 1985. Like the five-year-old who was helping his family stack bales of silage. One bale fell on him and he died.

Street trading is against the law for children under eighteen in the UK. But a Hertfordshire schoolboy was selling flowers on a busy main road when he was knocked down by a car – and killed.

The most common job amongst working teenagers is doing a paper round. But during the winter a boy in Bishop's Stortford was knocked off his bike and killed while working on his round.

These tragedies show that the rules and regulations about work and safety aren't just a load of red tape. They are for children's benefit. Nearly a third of working children suffer some kind of accident. One in ten have serious accidents.

The laws about health and safety at work were fought for in the past by people who saw how children and adults were being injured and killed at work. Unfortunately, health and safety standards are now dropping again. Young people at work and on training schemes are suffering more accidents as a result.

Yet in the developing world things are still as bad for children – or worse – than they were in this country's past. Children often work because they need food to survive. But the work they do uses up so much of their energy that they end up with serious malnutrition. This makes them more likely to catch infectious diseases.

Children in Brazil work on sugar-cane plantations from the age of seven. It is very hard work, but they get fed only a third of the calories they need. As a result their bodies may not ever develop properly, and they may also be mentally backward.

It damages children's bones when they have to work doubled up in carpet factories. It damages a child's eyesight to work for up to fourteen hours a day connecting fine wires in an eletronics factory. Dangerous machinery can maim and kill children at work. Dangerous chemicals can poison them.

It's bad for children's health to work in dark, airless factories without proper toilet facilities. It's bad for children to miss out on play times, meals times and exercise. It's depressing, but the fact remains that all over the world, work is harming children in many serious ways. Sometimes, it even kills them.

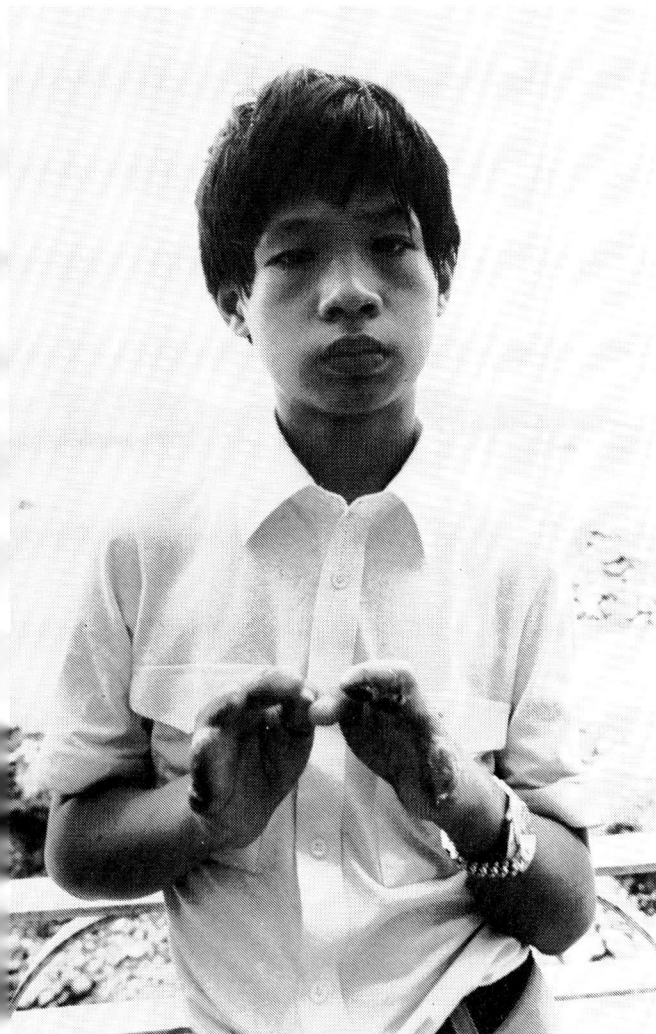

Left He's only fourteen, but this Hong Kong boy is already damaged for life by the loss of his fingers. He was working on a dangerous machine in a Hong Kong sweat-shop. His employer did not care enough – or would not pay – to provide for the necessary safety equipment. This is the result. Yet he's lucky in some respects: this boy has been adopted by a wealthy foster father.

Above No, it's not the Dark Ages. It's a recent picture of a boy mining coal in the South American state of Columbia. He has to drag up to one hundred kilos of coal along the shaft because it is too low to take carting equipment. Crawling with the lamp in his teeth all day is extremely hurtful to his physical health – not to mention his mental well-being. Add the risk of death and injury from working in a dark, underground mineshaft, and you'll see how dangerous child labour can really be.

Right Sunshine and smiles for this American boy in the southern states of the USA. The tractor he sits on in this tobacco field has a pretty sunshade on top. But what about protective bars or safety equipment? Working on a farm can be fun, but accidents can be fatal. Tractors can be especially dangerous. An English boy of fourteen was killed recently when he fell off the tractor he was driving and was crushed to death by the trailer. Trade unions have tried to raise the age at which children can drive tractors from 13 to 17, but employers won't agree.

Education: all work and no play?

Some children like school. Some children don't. But in the West, where everybody has to go to school, it's easy to forget what education really means for children.

The years before school was made compulsory were cruel years for children. In those days, children laboured long hours in mines and factories without any hope of escape. It was compulsory education that really put an end to the worst forms of child work – both in Britian and in the USA.

Of course children still work. But the longer they work, the less time they have for school and their own development. And the worse their school work is now, the less chance they have of escaping from badly paid, boring types of work in the future.

But good education isn't just for jobs – it's for life. Children need the opportunity to develop their personalities and other talents as well as their brains. School activities, like acting and art, can bring out a child's imagination and confidence. School sports and team games can help children learn co-operation and team work – as well as keeping them fit.

Of course not all education is geared to children's needs. The school system in Britain began with the Victorian idea that children should be taught strict obedience, in order to make them more useful workers of the future. Children were taken off the streets and put under adult authority. With the use of discipline and corporal punishment, they were trained to be punctual, careful and quiet.

Today there is still disagreement about whether children should be educated for their own development, or trained for work.

In contrast, most children in the developing world never get the chance of any education. Only a tiny minority get the schooling which might help them to escape exploitation. Parents of poor children tend to send them to work rather than to school. But it's no good blaming parents for doing that when their only other choice is to starve.

Parents and employers also need education – to show them how important it is for children to go to school. And when children have been to school, it is easier for them to know what their rights are, and to say 'no' to exploitation.

Right No chairs, desks, or tables – no classroom even. But this village school in India is still the best chance these children have of freeing themselves from poverty. If they can learn the skills of reading and writing, a whole new world will be opened to them. In the developing world, only the lucky ones go to school. Three-quarters of children never even get a chance to go to primary school. Those who do make it to school often have to drop out because they are needed by their families to work.

Right Of all children's jobs in Britain, a paper round is the most usual. That's because it is supposed to fit in well with education. The paper girl gets up early to do her job before school. Or else, she takes papers around after school so that she doesn't miss any lessons. She's only allowed to work a limited number of hours, so that she's not too tired for homework or schoolwork. Yet the discipline of being on time and responsible is also a good education for future employment, and having her own money is preparation for being adult too.

Below Education for these western children includes a lesson in mechanics. Because we live in a society which is so dependent upon machines, this is a chance to learn something practical which will be useful in day to day life. It may also be seen by a future employer as good training for a job in mechanics or engineering. Perhaps, too, it will help the girls escape from the prejudice that females can't fix their own cars or get their hands dirty! Maybe by the next lesson the girls will stop watching and start doing.

Exploiting children: a world-wide problem

What does it mean to 'exploit' a child's labour? Not everyone agrees on this. But generally, 'exploitation' means that a child's health, welfare and development should not be put at risk by an employer who makes an unfair profit from the child's work.

There are all sorts of reasons why children are exploited. Poverty is the root cause. Governments' social policies often add to this by making it impossible for people to climb out of poverty. Changes in the modern world, with more industry and less work in rural areas, have also meant people flocking to the cities – only to find unemployment and poverty.

Above This is Crossroads 'squatter camp' in Cape Town, South Africa. The children here live (or 'squat' against the law) in conditions of utter poverty. This is because of the Government's policy of apartheid. In South Africa, although Blacks work for white people they are not allowed to live near Whites. South Africa is a rich nation, but wages for Blacks are much lower than for Whites. As a result, many children start work young and don't get a decent education. This continues a situation where Whites live in comfort and Blacks live in poverty.

Traditional ideas about the role of women and children can also cause exploitation of girls. Girls are often expected to work in the home instead of going to school. This cuts the cost of having children for parents, and allows women to have still more. This adds

Left The tobacco industry is a huge multinational business. Cigarettes and cigars are sold at a great profit in the West – and increasingly in the Third World. Yet the people who do the work of growing the tobacco are mostly poor people of the developing world – like this boy in Argentina. He ties up the tobacco leaves to dry in the sun. Big multinationals make big money by using low-paid, casual labour, including children. This saves them the wage costs of well-paid and permanent staff.

to poverty, which adds to the exploitation of children – and so the cycle continues.

In many cases, children work in small craft workshops, factories and businesses. But it is the wealthiest companies in the world – the multinationals – who are the real employers at the end of a long chain of bosses and buyers.

By using labour in countries where poverty and the laws allow it, multinational companies can escape the restrictions of 150 years of anti-child labour laws in their own countries. They make and buy products very cheaply in the poorest parts of the world – often using children to manufacture them. Then they sell these products at many times the cost in the rich parts of the world.

The cigarette industry works on this basis, as well as the large craft export businesses – like carpet-making in Morocco and the clothing industry in the Far East.

Children here do the jobs by hand which would cost a lot in wages from a western workforce. It's even cheaper to employ children to do jobs by hand, than it is to buy machines to make the same products in the West.

The international trade union movement is organized to block this exploitation of children as part of their campaign against cheap labour everywhere.

Below This girl in Thailand is making umbrellas which will be sold to tourists or exported to the West. She and her friends work for low wages at young ages because they have barely enough money to survive. But the product they make is a pretty luxury, sold to rich people with money to spare for things they don't really need. The profits made will most likely go into the pockets of a rich western employer. By using child labour in the Third World, this employer gets around the laws at home which stop people from exploiting the young.

The law: a double-edged sword

If so many children all over the world are being exploited by employers, why not stop it by making it against the law?

The trouble is, most children work from tough necessity. If they don't work, they don't survive. For children like this, laws which ban them from working tip them out of the frying pan and into the fire.

Anyway, millions of children already work against the law. In Britain, there are laws which are meant to protect young people and children under 16 from working in poor and dangerous conditions. But they are being ignored and broken all the time.

Occasionally employers are fined for using child labour – like the Norfolk farmer who had to pay £1,000. He was found guilty of employing a fourteen-year-old for carrot-topping work with dangerous machines. Or the Deeside company fined £100 for using a sixteen-year-old to work a 22-hour shift. This girl's parents had given their consent to her working – which goes to show how difficult it can be to enforce laws against child work.

The law itself is in such a muddle that prosecutions are difficult to bring. Parliament has laid down the basic regulations, but local authorities provide the details of the law. This means that a child's job can be legal in London – where fifteen-year-olds can work for up to five hours on a Saturday. But the same job could be illegal in other parts of the country.

Most children who have jobs in Britain are working illegally. Sometimes this is because parents and employers don't know what the law is. They may be confused by the variations. Or their bosses may be deliberately breaking the law in order to cut their wage costs. The most common way in which the law is broken is through the failure to register children as working with the local authority.

Education Welfare Officers have to catch a child at work before they can take any legal action. Yet they have no right to enter work premises. Cases of children's labour often don't come to light until a child is injured in an accident at work.

Laws which make children's jobs illegal can also cut them off from the protection of the law. You can't run to a policeman to say your work is dangerous when you're not legally allowed to do that job in the first place. Nor can you complain about minimum wages, about not being in a trade union, or about being sacked unfairly, if your job is illegal.

Yet when the law is used together with other changes – like fighting poverty, raising adult wages and compulsory education – it can work very well. It was a combination of these changes together with new laws that put an end to the worst cases of child labour in Britain.

The International Labour Organization has long been pressing for changes in the law. They want to see an international law to make it illegal for any child to work before the school-leaving age, or before the age of fifteen.

Left This boy's job is to make the watering cans and other metal goods stacked outside his workshop. Should there be a law against it? Chinese culture is so different from ours that we can't say whether a law banning his work would help him. When children are working because of poverty, stopping them from working can mean worse poverty. And for children who carry on working despite the law, it means they have no rights or protection from the law if injured or badly treated. Anyway, who are we to say that children of other countries should not work?

Right In Britain, only adults get to wear such official-looking uniforms. Children just aren't given this kind of official authority. But in Brazil, this young parking attendant is only thirteen years old. Different countries have different ideas about when childhood turns into adulthood. In the poorer countries, childhood is much shorter than in the West, because children often have to work from a very early age. Poverty and other complicated factors all add to the reasons why children have to work. Those aren't things that the law – on its own – can change.

Left This British boy is here because he wants to be. His work is helping out at a saddle-makers. He gives his labour without being paid. But in exchange, he gets the chance to ride the horses also kept here. It's an arrangement that suits him and suits the saddle-maker. Yet if he wanted to do this as a regular, paid job, that would be against the law. That law goes back decades, and is designed to stop him from missing out on school by working too late or too early, or from working too many hours in the day. What's more, the workroom here seems a cosy place to help out: but as an environment for an employee, it's hardly up to scratch.

Children are the future

Not all children work because they have to. But most of them do. So banning all child labour wouldn't help those children – even if it were possible.

What can be changed are the causes behind child labour, like poverty. Most children work because there simply isn't enough money in the family. Unemployment and low wages for adults often mean children are forced to earn. If their parents had jobs with a decent living wage – that would set many a child free from hard work.

As most child labour is in the developing world, this would take a huge international commitment to change. At present, the rich world squeezes money out of the poor world through using its resources and its labour, including child labour. The powerful and rich countries of the developed world would have to show a real desire to change the system.

Many people in the West do care, and have raised money for the Third World. But only a few of the governments of the richer countries are giving the amount of money in aid recommended by the United Nations. And 'aid' isn't always used in the most helpful ways. Developing nations need money which goes to help their poor people. But often the West gives aid as a bank loan to the poor world and then expects high repayments which cripple the country being 'helped'.

Below These Madagascar children are learning about agriculture in the garden of their local school. For them it's not just a hobby. The skills they pick up here could bring a life of independence – instead of poverty. The school is funded by the international organization for children UNICEF. Like other aid agencies, UNICEF sees the way to end child exploitation in schemes which combine education with work. This gardening lesson will give the children valuable experience: it will also bring them a crop of food!

Left Proud and happy after their fund-raising run, these children put their arms around each other's shoulders. And by raising money for the victims of poverty in the Third World, they are also reaching out to less fortunate children. These days all of us are becoming more aware that it's one world we live in. When we can change greedy attitudes in the rich West, then we can start to fight the poverty that lies behind the exploitation of children everywhere.

So many, many changes are needed to end the exploitation of children at work. One of these changes would have to be free education for all children. Changes in laws all over the world would also help – if these went together with other changes.

Another way to make changes is to stop buying the goods that children make or work on. If people refused to buy the tea picked by Indian children, you can be sure the people who run the tea trade would take notice!

The trade union movement all over the world is working hard to stamp out the exploitation of children. The recession which affects the whole world doesn't help, as adult unemployment and poverty mean more child work. The technological advances which put more adults out of work are a problem too. But when trade unions fight for good wages and jobs for adults, they are also fighting to end child labour.

Another way that people are trying to bring change is by arguing for the rights of children. The idea is to look at the whole of children's lives, to consider their needs, and how adults have a duty to safeguard them.

If children can enjoy and benefit from work without losing their right to education, health, play and love – then well and good. But if work is putting children's welfare and their future in danger – then it must be stopped.

After all, the future of the whole world depends on today's children. Many things can wait for change – but children cannot.

Reference

These days many people think the best way to stop the abuse of child workers is to stand up for children's rights. These rights were set out in this declaration by the United Nations in 1959.

The Rights of the Child

1. The right to equality, regardless of race, colour, sex, religion, national or social origin.
2. The right to develop physically and mentally in a healthy manner.
3. The right to a name and nationality.
4. The right to adequate nutrition, housing and medical services.
5. The right to special care, if handicapped.
6. The right to love, understanding and protection.
7. The right to free education, to play and recreation.
8. The right to be among the first to receive relief in times of disaster.
9. The right to protection against all forms of neglect, cruelty and exploitation.
10. The right to be brought up in a spirit of tolerance, peace and universal brotherhood.

A Children's Charter

There are different rules all over Britain to say what work children can and can't do. But this is a guide to the sort of regulations which are in force in most places. It is taken from the Avon 'children's charter' – but contact your own county's Education Department to find out about the by-laws affecting children's work in your area.

1. You aren't allowed to work until you are thirteen years old – unless you are helping your parents in farming or gardening.
2. You can only work for two hours each day on schooldays.
3. You can't work before school, except to do newspaper or milk rounds. These must be done between 7:00 and 8:00 a.m.
4. Stop work before 7:00 p.m. If you work in the morning too, it has to be for the same employer – such as a newsagent.
5. You are allowed to work in school holidays and on Saturdays for up to four hours.
6. On Sundays you can work for two hours between 7:00 a.m. and 10:00 a.m., except on farms.
7. Don't work more than twenty hours a week.
8. It is against the law for you to work in: pubs, clubs, snooker parlours, tobacconists, chemists, betting shops, fair grounds, abattoirs.
9. You can't work at any machine described as dangerous under the Offices, Shops and Premises Act of 1963.
10. Even if you aren't paid, it counts as work if you 'help out' – in a relative's business for instance.

Useful organizations

The Anti-Slavery Society: This is the world's oldest human rights organization, founded in 1839. It speaks up for the powerless millions of people across the world – including children – who work as slaves. The Anti-Slavery Society produces leaflets, information, a Newsletter and a series of publications about child labour (see Further reading list). Anti-Slavery Society, 18 Brixton Road, London SW9 6AT
Tel: 01 582 4040

Child Poverty Action Group: A campaigning organization which works to end child poverty in Britain. As poverty is at the root of child labour, the CPAG helps to stop the exploitation of children. It produces many publications and information leaflets, plus a journal called *Poverty*. Child Poverty Action Group, 1 Macklin Street, London WC2 5NH   Tel: 01 242 3225

Children's Legal Centre: This is an independent organization concerned with law and policy as it affects children and young people in England and Wales. The Centre aims for the recognition of young people as individuals who need to play a full part in the decisions which affect their lives. The Centre publishes the monthly magazine *Childright*, full of interesting but detailed articles about the law and children. Children's Legal Centre, 20 Compton Terrace, London N1 2UN
Tel: 01 359 6251

Health and Safety Commission: Its job is to protect the health, safety and welfare of people at work – including children – and of people affected by the risks which may result from that work. Health and Safety Commission, Regina House, 259 Old Marylebone Road, London NW1 5RR
Tel: 01 723 1262

International Labour Organization: This is a UN agency which seeks to promote social justice all over the world by promoting humane conditions at work. It is the main body pressing for minimum age regulations below which children would not be allowed to work, to be agreed all over the world. Since it began in 1919, the ILO has been concerned with the issue of child labour. It produces a wide variety of publications and reports. ILO London Office, 96–98 Marsham Street, London SW1P 4LY   Tel: 01 828 6401

International Labour Organization (Headquarters), CH 1211, Geneva 22, Switzerland.

Low Pay Unit: A campaigning body fighting for the rights of the low paid – which also means many children in this country. It produces many publications and information leaflets as well as exhibitions and posters (see Futher reading list for reports on children's work in Britain). Low Pay Unit, 9 Upper Berkeley Street, London W1H 8BY Tel: 01 626 7278/9

Trade Union Congress: This body puts the views of the trade union movement to the government and to the general public. It represents nearly a hundred British trade unions with some 10 million members. As such it is the biggest group defending the rights of workers – and so it is deeply concerned about the issue of child labour. The TUC produces many publications and provides information and practical help in workers' rights. Trade Union Congress, Congress House, Great Russell Street, London WC1B 3L5.

UNICEF: This international organization is the United Nation's Children's Fund. It has many and various projects around the world to improve the plight of children, including child labourers. It produces many reports and publications (see Further reading list). UK Committee for UNICEF, 55 Lincoln's Inn Field, London WC2A 3NB Tel: 01 405 5592

Further reading

NON-FICTION

At What Age Can I? from the Children's Legal Centre (see Useful organizations). A booklet which tells you what the law allows you to do, and at what age.

All Work and No Play: Child Labour Today A TUC Resource Book, produced by the TUC and UNICEF. Published by the TUC. Available from the UK Committee for UNICEF (see Useful organizations).

Anti-Slavery Society Series on *Child Labour* These in-depth reports cover
1. Child Labour in Morocco's Carpet Industry
2. Child Labour in India
3. Child Labour in Spain
4. Child Labour in Italy
5. Child Labour in Thailand
6. Child Labour in Jamaica
7. Child Labour in South Africa

Child Workers Today by James Challis and David Ellman is also available from the Anti-Slavery Society.

A Child's World: A Social History of English Childhood 1800–1914 by James Walvin (Penguin 1982).

Development and Change Vol. 13, No. 4. 'Child Workers', by Sage Publications. A collection of academic essays on child labour around the world.

The Rights of Children, edited by Robert Franklin (Blackwell). A serious, in-depth study of children's rights today.

Working Children from the Low Pay Unit (see Useful organizations). This is a detailed report about working children in Britain.

FICTION

Two classic works of British fiction which give an insight into the lives of child workers in our past are:

Oliver Twist, by Charles Dickens

The Waterbabies, by Charles Kingsley.

44

Index